THE POWER
TO PERSUADE?

Also available in the Pioneer *Perspectives* series:

THE POWER TO PERSUADE?

The Media and the Church

Cleland Thom

WORD PUBLISHING
Nelson Word Ltd
Milton Keynes, England

WORD AUSTRALIA
Kilsyth, Victoria, Australia

NELSON WORD CANADA
Vancouver, B.C., Canada

STRUIK CHRISTIAN BOOKS (PTY) LTD
Cape Town, South Africa

JOINT DISTRIBUTORS SINGAPORE—
ALBY COMMERCIAL ENTERPRISES PTE LTD
and
CAMPUS CRUSADE, ASIA LTD

PHILIPPINE CAMPUS CRUSADE FOR CHRIST
Quezon City, Philippines

CHRISTIAN MARKETING NEW ZEALAND LTD
Havelock North, New Zealand

JENSCO LTD
Hong Kong

SALVATION BOOK CENTRE
Malaysia

THE POWER TO PERSUADE?

ISBN 0-85009-735-5

Unless otherwise indicated, Scripture quotations are from the HOLY BIBLE, NEW INTERNATIONAL VERSION, copyright © 1973, 1978, 1984 by International Bible Society.

Front cover illustration: *Farms Near Auvers, late July 1890*, Vincent Van Gogh, courtesy of Tate Gallery, London/Bridgeman Art Gallery (detail).

Reproduced, printed and bound in Great Britain for Nelson Word Ltd. by Cox & Wyman Ltd., Reading.

94 95 96 97 / 10 9 8 7 6 5 4 3 2 1

FOREWORD

Pioneer *Perspectives* are perhaps more than their title suggests!

They are carefully researched presentations of material, on important issues, appealing to thinking churches, creative leaders and responsible Christians.

Each *Perspective* pioneers in as much as it is at the cutting edge of biblical and theological issues. Each will continue to pioneer with new ideas, concepts and data drawn from Scripture, history and a contemporary understanding of both.

They are perspectives in as much as they aim to be an important contribution to the ongoing debate on issues such as women in ministry and leadership; prophets and prophecy in the church; biblical models of evangelism; integrating and discipling new believers; growing and building local churches and further perspectives on Christ's second coming.

Importantly, these studies use a journal style of presentation, and are written by people who are currently working out the implications of the issues they are writing about, in local churches. This is vital if we are to escape the dangerous fantasy of abstract theology without practical experience. They are not written to contribute to the paralysis of analysis—rather to feed, strengthen, nurture and inform so that we can be equipped to get God's will done, by networking the nations with the gospel using all the resources that are available to us.

God's Word is always an event. How much we thank Him that He has left us an orderly account of what He wants us to believe, how He wants us to live, and what He wants us to do in order to bring heaven to the earth. As we embrace a better understanding of Scripture, rooted in local church, national and international mission, we shall become a part of the great eschatological purpose of bringing back the King—not for a church defeated, cowering and retiring but for one which, despite colossal odds, pressures and persecutions, is faithful to her Lord and His Word. To do that we must 'search the Scriptures' to see if many of these 'new things' are true. I commend these *Perspectives* to you as they are published on a regular basis throughout these coming years.

Gerald Coates
Director Pioneer Trust/Team Leader

*This book is dedicated to my wife Rachael
and my boys, Oliver and Barnaby.
They've all been really good news to me!*

Pioneer consists of a team and network of churches, committed to dynamic and effective biblical Christianity.

The national team act as advisers and consultants to churches, which in many cases develop into a partnership with the Pioneer team. These are the churches keen to identify with the theology, philosophy, ethos and purpose of Pioneer. The team have a vigorous youth ministry, church-planting strategy and evangelistic emphasis.

Training courses include Equipped to Lead, Emerging Leaders and the highly successful TIE teams (Training In Evangelism).

Pioneer have also been instrumental in initiating and funding March for Jesus (with Ichthus/YWAM); Jubilee Campaign (for the suffering church worldwide); and ACET (Aids Care Education Training).

CONTENTS

INTRODUCTION

It was a hot Friday afternoon. As editor of a weekly local newspaper in London, I was busy drawing up schedules for the following week. The phone rang. The voice on the other end was chilling.

'If you don't retract your story on page one of this week's paper, you'll die.'

Since the story was a stinging attack on a terrorist group, it sounded as though the caller might have the power to act on his threat. And although he didn't either get his retraction or finish me off, the call made an important point: the press wields enormous power in people's lives. Quite simply, our thinking on many issues is probably shaped more by the media than it is by the Bible!

In the past, most Christians have tended to be armchair critics when it comes to the media. We've been quick to complain—and even pray—about what we don't like. But I believe now is the time for us to stop grumbling and to start having a voice in the newspapers and on the airwaves.

Last year the well-known television news reader Martin Lewis caused a stir by calling for more good news in the media. He had a point—and presented us an opportunity on a plate. If we can't be bearers of good news, then who can? And in doing so, we can begin to create a climate that will ensure that our evangelistic activities are better received.

That's the reason for this book. In it I've tried to state the case for having a church with a high media profile, and I've also attempted to be practical in telling you how to go about it, with no cost and little risk. The rest is up to you!

Cleland Thom
Chichester, June 1994

CHAPTER 1

A SPITTING IMAGE?

The Church's Relationship with the Media

The only time many churches hit the headlines is when the vicar runs off with the choirmistress! And what do we do about it? The same as politicians, the same as Royalty, that's what. We blame the press.

But that's a cop-out. It's easy to sit back and moan about bad publicity or no publicity. But we need to ask ourselves: what are we doing to change the situation? Are we informing the press of what we're doing in a way that is interesting, relevant and up to date? And are we, in fact, doing anything particularly newsworthy anyway? If we're not, then we shouldn't complain when the publicity isn't what we'd like it to be.

Happily, the church has changed enormously over the last ten years. New churches abound, denominational churches are gurgling with new wine and both have a real desire to get the church off the Top Secret list and into the community with a gospel which ordinary people—*Sun* readers—hear gladly, the same as Jesus did.

However, despite this change in emphasis, many churches still do a Howard Hughes impression when it comes to using the press to communicate with the public. Yes, there are risks, but that applies to anything useful that we do for God. We need to grasp the fact that the benefits outweigh the risks.

The problem is, however, that we still haven't shaken off our bad public image from the past. The press still sees us either as an out-of-date, ineffective religious institution or a semicredible, sect-like group of tongue-speaking weirdos who seem to be against more than they're for.

Newspapers are among the primary shapers of public opinion these days. They can unseat presidents—ask Richard Nixon of America. They can destroy reputations—ask the Duchess of York. They can shape morality—for better, but usually for worse. And in this situation, we as the church can do one of two things. We can either sit back and complain as the media misuses its influence and bombards people with godless garbage. Or we can step out of our ghettos and learn how to use the newspapers' influence to advance God's kingdom on the earth.

Taking the latter route is risky. We may be accused of using worldly methods to carry out the King's business. But the same criticism has been levelled at Cliff Richard and others who are bold enough to dare to present the gospel in the world's arena. I believe that people should be picking up their papers and reading about us—about our church and about our God.

God's PR strategy

In the Old Testament, the prophets demonstrated and communicated their message in the most extraordinary ways. I'm not sure whether Isaiah would have qualified as one of the *Sun's* page 7 fellahs, but he *did* walk around naked for three years to make God's point to the nation. I've no doubt that he'd have made the tabloids if they'd been around in those days! Imagine the headlines:

AND NOW FOR THE BAD NUDES—PROPHET
GIVES THE BARE FACTS.

Jesus managed to avoid *courting* publicity, and yet handled mass adulation wisely when it came. On the one hand, He was born into an obscure nation and avoided going to Rome, the obvious place to find a mass audience. And there *were* times when He was as good at dodging the crowds as the Invisible Man and told the demoniac to say 'No Comment' after He delivered him.

On the other hand, He told His people to be like a city on a hill. You can't get much more noticeable than that! And He frequently made a point of turning *to* the crowds to make controversial statements, and performed miracles in key public places. In other words, He avoided becoming a media figure for the sake of it, but wasn't afraid of big audiences and used mass publicity wisely when He needed to.

You can see the same attitude in the New Testament church. Peter could have run back into the Upper Room after the outpouring of the Holy Spirit at Pentecost—but he didn't! He turned and faced the crowds. Philip didn't hesitate to conduct miracles among the masses in Samaria. And although Paul spent a lot of time working in synagogues, he also went public on many occasions, going to the river in Philippi, to the market place in Athens and to the lecture hall in Ephesus.

If the biblical pattern for God's people was to have a high public profile at times, then surely we need to follow it, using every opportunity that our culture offers us.

We need to start regarding the press as an opportunity, not an obstacle, and begin to influence it—wisely and professionally. If we want to invade every seam and strata of society with the gospel of God, then surely the press must be near the top of our agenda. For when we communicate through the press, we don't just help to shape them—we can also influence thousands, even millions of their readers!

Hopefully by the end of this book you'll have a better idea of how it can be done—and done well, without taking too many risks.

CHAPTER 2

NO NEWS IS BAD NEWS

What the Press are Looking For

A vicar I used to know knew how to get his church into print. Week in, week out, his controversial comments on homosexuality, women, under-age sex, drugs and virtually any other subject you could think of appeared in his local paper, often on the front page. (He made sure the copy arrived on the day of the week when news was short!) This was one way of getting a church—and God—into print, and this vicar built up a big following for his church as a result.

Publicising your church *can* be just as easy! Churches and local papers have two important things in common.

Firstly, they both have a desire to reach the whole community, aiming to cross all social, racial and cultural divides, and appeal to both sexes and all age groups.

Secondly, they are both interested in 'Good News'— what we prefer to call the gospel. There is a growing trend among local papers these days to major on 'Good News'. The argument is that because there is so much doom and gloom around, with front pages usually full of stories about violent crimes, newspapers should try to cheer people up a bit.

And this is where we, the church, come in! If we aren't capable of producing Good News, then who is? Let's examine some of the types of potential story that are likely to be staring you in the face in most churches:

1. Human interest stories

These are basically stories about *ordinary people with a story to tell*. The scope is endless.

Personal testimonies are an obvious example. A mother who has been healed of agoraphobia and can now go shopping normally; a drug addict who has been freed of his habit without any withdrawal symptoms; a homosexual man who is now married with children after receiving prayer; a woman diagnosed childless who has just had her first child—many Christians nowadays have powerful stories to tell. And why not tell them?

A few years ago, when I was freelancing for the *News of the World*, they regularly rang me up and asked: 'Have you got any good Christian testimonies?' They knew the impact of these stories, just as John did when he wrote, 'They shall overcome . . . by the word of their testimony.'

Obviously, we need to take great care when we decide to go public with someone's testimony! We must make sure that the story is genuine—that God has actually done what we say He has done. Sadly, a lot of healing testimonies these days don't really stand up to medical scrutiny. From the press point of view, a person is either healed or they aren't. They won't be particularly impressed if a deaf person still can't hear but is 'walking out their healing until it is manifested', or is claiming that they're healed and that contrary symptoms are 'lies of the devil'! Statements like these do God a bad service. When Jesus healed people, they were healed—and He didn't mind who checked.

Similarly, we need to make sure the person involved is properly settled and rooted into church life and can cope with the implications of appearing in the paper. What will their friends, families and employers think? Could the story make them proud? Have they really left their pasts behind them? After all, there's little glory for God if the local paper carries a story about a drug addict who is miraculously freed of his habit one week, but is back on heroin again three weeks later.

We obviously need to be cautious—but not to the point where we never leave the starting blocks!

Stories about *human achievement* are also popular. Perhaps you've got a dyslexic boy in your church who's passed his A-level English after being prayed for; or a disabled person who is taking part in the London Marathon to raise money for fellow sufferers. People love to hear how other people succeed against the odds.

Churches should also have no problem in finding stories about *people who care for others* in some way. Obviously none of us want to become proud or perform our good works just to get recognition. However, a story about the kids who gave away their Christmas presents to needy children in a home would have tremendous appeal. So would a piece about the 90-year-old lady in your congregation who serves up dinner to people 20 years her junior at an old folk's luncheon club each week; or the person who's been doing the soup run to the city's homeless regularly now for ten years.

It's a good idea to go through copies of national and local tabloid papers and see how many human interest stories you can find. There will probably be more than you'd expect. You'll notice that few of them involve anybody famous. That's the joy of human interest stories! They involve ordinary, everyday people—the kinds of people in our churches.

2. Social action

Social action is back on the agenda in most churches these days—and a good thing too! And social action programmes provide excellent opportunities for newspaper stories because they present the church in a caring role. Next time your church initiates a project aimed at helping the needy or the environment, remember there's probably a story there somewhere. Maybe some of your people are going to clean rubbish out of a stream; or paint an old people's day centre; or test sea water for pollution; or collect ten thousand tins of beans to send to Romania; or open a new hostel for the homeless; or meet local councillors to ask for better facilities for the disabled. All these ideas can present excellent story and picture opportunities for your local paper, and even local radio and television.

3. General news

A good public profile takes a long time to build up. A bad one can be achieved in a day! If the vicar runs off with the choir mistress, that church will get national profile straight away—and will probably still be tainted with the reputation five years later. Creating a *good* public perception of your church could take you around ten years, and newer churches may find it takes longer.

The main outlet for a church's news is the local paper, which tends to prefer something that is *familiar*. That's why a lifeless denominational church is far more likely to get its press releases used in the paper than the house church round the corner. St Pomegranate's might be dead—but it does have an aura of credibility about it as far as the local press is concerned.

Newer churches love to change things, and there's nothing wrong with that! The last thing we want is tradition and routine. However, we need to remember that people can be suspicious of anything that's unfamiliar, so we must find ways to use the press to help us present our changes in a positive, interesting way.

One way all churches can build a better public profile is to aim to get something in the paper every week. In fact, news is happening all the time—if you learn how to recognise it. The Christmas panto, the summer play scheme, the mothers and toddlers' club coffee morning, the cheque presentation to the local branch of Oxfam, the church member who's just written a book, gone to Romania, returned from Romania, been appointed leader, retired, celebrated a golden wedding, taken over as school governor or even died—all these qualify as news and are worth a paragraph or two in the local paper.

Here's a more comprehensive list of news items that are common in most churches:

1. Announcing events.
2. Reporting on the success of the events.
3. Comments from leaders on items in the national news.
4. Unusual incidents which happen to members.
5. Changes in leadership.
6. Membership trends.
7. Specific projects/activities.

We need to regard anything and everything we do as news if it has a public aspect to it. If people read about us in the paper week in, week out, we'll be sowing seeds of credibility and respectability—and as we all know, we will reap what we sow, if we're patient.

4. Information

Most local or national newspapers nowadays are joining a current trend towards *information marketing*. The days when papers just contained news are fading. They now carry information about duty chemists, emergency contact numbers, help lines, details of road works, transport services, the weather and columns of diary items ranging from jumble sales to yoga classes.

We should analyse our local papers, see what kind of

information they print and send in the appropriate items. Most churches are likely to have entries for the diary page—remember, send in details of *every* public meeting or event. Some churches may run advice lines, counselling centres and social action/emergency services which qualify for inclusion in the help lines.

These, then, are the general areas of church activity which are likely to make the local news. You may be able to think of others. Try sitting down and listing all the possible stories that could be found within your church. You might be surprised how many you find!

CHAPTER 3

TAKE A LETTER, MR EDITOR

Using the Letters Page

Who was one the most influential people in Britain during the 1970s? Edward Heath? Joe Gormley? Harold Wilson?

No. Mr R. K. Belsher, of Brighton! His claim to fame was that he had more letters published on local papers' letters pages than anyone else in the country.

He didn't just write to his own local paper, the *Brighton Argus*. He regularly wrote to scores of papers up and down the country. I remember working on London's *Islington Gazette* at the time and scarcely a week went by without a tome from RKB arriving in the post—and eventually appearing in the paper. His views on a whole range of subjects became legend throughout the land.

The local paper's letters page is one of the most important public forums in any town, surpassed only by the council chamber. And it's probably the *only* place where Mr Average can voice his views, not just to several thousand readers but also to the people who matter.

Speak to any local paper editor and he'll tell you that the letters page is one of the most important pages in the paper. It is eagerly read, and noted, by councillors, local government officials and just about everybody in a position of power, influence and authority. Any politician will tell you that the letters page helps them to gauge local feeling on current issues.

Silence isn't golden

Sadly, though, churches are not always represented in this vital forum.

I used to be editor of a large group of local papers in London with a readership of 350,000 and I often used to despair at the absence of a Christian voice on the letters pages. Important issues were often discussed and cried out for the views of the local churches, but the silence was deafening! Mediums, atheists, witches, pressure groups— they were only too quick to write in. But Christians? You rarely heard from them. I even went as far as meeting some church leaders to encourage them to mobilise their people to write, but still very little happened. There were even times when I stuck my neck right out and wrote very pro-Christian views in my 'Editor's View' column—and then received little support from fellow Christians on the letters page when the anti-mail came flooding in. 'Just goes to show how much support your opinions really have,' one of my directors once told me. Even though I knew he was wrong, it was very hard to argue with him. Perhaps some of us need to say a quick 'Sorry' to God for not being salt and light in this vital forum!

So what can Christians and churches write about? Well, we can either *start* a debate—or join one.

Starting a debate

If we want to start a debate, the list of subjects is endless: abortion, Sunday trading, embryology, pornography, child abuse, women's rights, homeless, the environment, lone-parent families—these are all subjects on which Christians may have a viewpoint. Of course there may also be specific local issues which we can raise, and we can become a rallying point in the community. Maybe facilities for the disabled are very inadequate in your town. Or perhaps there is an environmental eyesore which needs attention, or a dangerous road which needs a lollipop patrol. These are all issues where a lively, outward-looking church could rally the community, through the letters page, to achieve some common good. And of course as we do so, our public image will improve, hopefully with plenty of opportunities to share the gospel cropping up along the way.

While I was helping to lead a church in London, we became involved in a number of educational, cultural and moral local issues, and even helped to change some ungodly council policy—all by getting people to write letters to the local paper. People who were keen on letter writing were trained and then watched out for important issues. Then they talked them through with their leaders, put pen to paper—and waited for the response. One letter on a controversial issue caused an uproar, and prompted public meetings, mass demonstrations and other militant responses—all part of standing up for what you believe in! Questions were asked in the council chamber, and eventually a piece of anti-Christian legislation was dropped. That's the power of the church working through the press!

Clearly, though, churches must choose their issues wisely. It's easy for us to simply pick up the 'right-wing agenda', but we need to broaden our focus and speak out on issues of social justice, too.

We must also make sure we aren't seen to be writing simply to protect our evangelical corner or our own vested interests. It's been said before that the church is the only organisation which exists for the benefit of its nonmembers. However, in reality it's easy to forget this. Many churches would be happy to write to the local paper about 'Keeping Sunday Special'. How keen would they be, however, to support the local gay community in trying to get an advice centre established? It would be sad if we ended up hijacking the letters page for our own evangelical ends and forgetting the community whom we have a duty to love.

Entering an existing debate

We can also join in debates that are running already. Interested church members should scan the local papers each week and look out for the hot issues, either on the letters page, in the news columns or in the editor's leader column. These aren't hard to find! There are always controversies raging of one kind or another, and we should select the ones where a Christian voice is needed and write the appropriate response—again, with a church leader's input.

We need to recognise, though, that not all issues are *church* issues. Some of them are personal—and one church member might have a different opinion to another. If Mrs Bloggs wants to write in support of her local council's stance on housing—fine! And if Mr Smith, a member of her house group, wishes to write with a contrary viewpoint, even better! A healthy church will be one which allows people room to disagree. The last thing we want is a 'party line'. Hopefully Mrs Bloggs and Mr Smith will have fellowship together before putting pen to paper, and will avoid personal animosity at all costs. Apart from that, however, they should both be free to express their opinions.

Church issues are different, however. There may be some issues where a whole church wishes to take a stand, and at times like these, coordination and accountability to leadership are critically important. It could be damaging to churches if people wrote letters on a church issue that the leaders either weren't aware of or weren't particularly happy about. Letters to the press can occasionally provoke considerable reaction which may affect other Christians. We are responsible to one another—we're a body—and we can't afford to have too many Lone Rangers in such a sensitive sphere. Even the Lone Ranger had Tonto!

Letter-writing campaigns

There may be situations when a letter-writing campaign is necessary. In general, I'm not very keen on campaigns, since editors are quick to spot them and see them for what they are. Having said that, I know that serious issues may occasionally arise which we want to take hold of corporately. There's certainly no better way of demonstrating the strength of feeling on an issue than by deluging the editor with mail!

Again, though, we need to avoid jumping on evangelical bandwagons or being perceived as protecting our own vested interests. Our focus should always be towards the community.

However, if we decide to run a coordinated campaign, we should try to make sure that people are left to express their views in their own way. Editors will not pay much attention to fifty letters from one church which are all virtually identical.

So let's get writing! The columns are open to us—in fact many local papers struggle to fill their letters pages at times! Let's start to identify the issues that are on God's heart, and get them into print.

Advice on how to write a letter will be given later in this book (see chapter 12).

CHAPTER 4

ALL CHANGE, PLEASE!

Campaigning Through the Press

The newspaper industry has been devastated by the recession during recent years. Local papers have suffered particularly badly. Dozens of titles have folded and thousands of jobs have been lost. Circulations have plummeted. So has revenue.

There's nothing like a bit of hardship to focus the thinking, and during the tough times, the newspapers which have survived have been forced to examine all kinds of new ideas to try and protect their circulations.

One particularly successful idea has been newspaper campaigns. Newspapers have moved away from simply reporting news. They now see their brief as making it, too. And I believe that churches can have a big part to play in aiding, and even initiating, newspaper campaigns. If we aren't the people equipped to bring change to society, then who are? The benefits, both in terms of public perception and in fighting injustice, are enormous.

What is a campaign?

The essence of a newspaper campaign is that it *makes something happen*. Editors like them because they raise the paper's profile, and gain attention, goodwill, credibility and extra sales. And it goes without saying that groups like churches who are also involved in the campaign stand to benefit, too.

Campaigns tend to fall into four categories: righting wrongs; forcing the authorities to change their minds; spurring on voluntary effort; and pointing the finger of blame. The most successful ones champion the interests of the ordinary people.

Last year the *Southampton Advertiser* ran an award-winning campaign called 'Filling the Empties'. It was an initiative aimed at spotting empty council homes and using them to house homeless families. Readers were mobilised to look out for empty properties and the local council was then urged to place homeless families in them.

The campaign ran for several months and was an enormous success—not just from the paper's point of view, but for the homeless, too: scores of them were housed as a result. Imagine the prestige that churches could have reaped had they been in partnership with the paper on such a key social issue!

The *Thurrock Gazette* in Essex also turned up trumps with an anti-drugs campaign. The paper was so concerned with the drugs problem in its town that it set out to unite the community by declaring Thurrock a drugs-free zone.

They got the backing of local firms who paid for information packs, posters, stickers and badges. The paper itself sponsored a police drugs line and helped organise leaflet and poster competitions, a youth club quiz, a seminar for teachers and a video of an anti-drugs play. It also ran a series of informative articles in the paper each week.

The campaign was so successful the Essex Police Committee decided to use it as a role model, and agreed to make funds available.

Again, imagine the opportunities for a church in a campaign like this. Many churches are working in the field of drugs nowadays and have had the resources to play a significant part.

Opportunities for the church

During my days as an editor, I managed to involve churches in some campaigns that my papers ran—with considerable success. One involved getting food and medical supplies shipped to Albania. The paper printed appeals for donations and the churches helped by collecting them and providing premises in which to store them. The initiative didn't involve too much time and effort, but the publicity and the prestige the churches received was enormous.

I also managed to get churches involved in my papers' campaigns during the Gulf War. These initiatives were so successful that Kuwait's daily paper the *Voice of Kuwait* ran a whole-page feature on them. Churches were involved by offering counselling and other services to people affected by the war in some way.

The most successful campaign, however, was the Peace Pals Project, run by my newspapers and the Evangelical Alliance. The idea was forge links between British and Iraqi children after the Gulf War. The papers printed a letter of goodwill, in Arabic, from a British child to an Iraqi one. Young British readers cut it out and sent it to the paper, with their photograph and a donation of one pound.

We gathered up the letters and forwarded them to the EA, who made sure that they were passed to Iraqi children. The money was sent to relief groups working among the young in the war-torn country.

Hundreds of British children took part, and some of them received replies. The prestige both we and the EA received was enormous. John Major praised it as an imaginative scheme and President Bush said it was very worthwhile. It was a genuine example of how the media could work with Christian groups to provide help for the needy and build bridges of reconciliation after a war.

These examples will give you an idea of the potential

that exists for local newspaper campaigns. And there's no reason on earth—or in heaven!—why churches shouldn't be playing their part in them.

Why doesn't your church try to initiate a campaign by thinking of a good idea and presenting it to the editor of your local paper? Here are some of the spheres you might consider.

Campaign ideas

Campaigns are usually well-supported if they are carefully selected. The most successful ones tend to be those with the potential to *benefit a significant number of readers*, those which involve *matters of life and death*, or *the health and welfare of children*. Issues that are boring or which alienate large groups of readers are to be avoided at all costs.

A good example would be a campaign to save the children's cancer ward at the local hospital—especially if your church secretary happened to be the ward sister. Another would be to aim to collect 10,000 toys for children in residential homes at Christmas.

The best way of identifying a campaign is to ask your church members: what are the issues that affect them? What are they concerned about? The chances are that between them, they'll be able to point to some possible ideas.

How to make an approach

Once you've come up with a good idea, you need to decide what resources you as a church can offer. The paper may give you the space, but if it is working in partnership with you, it is likely to look to you for voluntary help, money, administrative support, etc. The church's job isn't just to think up a bright idea for a campaign, but to play a leading part in running it.

Once you've got everything together, you need to put your proposals into a brief, simple and readable form and send them to your local paper's editor.

Here's an example of what a letter from Mugthorpe Christian Fellowship to Mr Gavin Smithers, editor of the *Mugthorpe Bugle*, might look like.

Dear Mr Smithers,

We are writing to ask if you would be interested in joining us in running a campaign in Mugthorpe to collect 10,000 toys for children in social services homes this Christmas.

All we are asking you for is the publicity—we would actually administer the campaign. This is how it would work:

You would run stories about the appeal every week during November, inviting your readers to support it. You would also print a list of places where toys could be deposited—church buildings throughout the town.

We would collect the toys, grade them according to suitability for sex and age and wrap them.

We would then provide a nicely decorated open-sided van, complete with a Father Christmas, to tour the town and take the presents to five different children's homes, which have been nominated to us by the council. The Mayor has already said that he would be keen to join in the delivery run—and may consider dressing up as Father Christmas himself.

Such a campaign would probably yield several good story and picture opportunities for you and would help us with our caring role in the community. We could find an appropriate name and design a logo using both your name and ours.

We would be prepared to fund the campaign and provide all volunteer help and administrative support.

We hope you will look on the idea enthusiastically.

Yours sincerely etc.

You get the idea? A campaign like this would help the church fulfil its caring role in society. And with sufficient prayer and spiritual warfare, the evangelistic opportunities and benefits in terms of contacts and public profile could be incalculable.

With more and more local papers becoming keen on campaigns and often struggling to find new ones, we should seize the opportunity to express God's heart to the community.

CHAPTER 5

GOD-SMACKED ... OR GOB-SMACKED?

Using the Press for Evangelism

Many church leaders feel they don't get their fair crack of the whip when it comes to press coverage of evangelism. Now some of the criticism is justified, but perhaps we need to look at the situation from the press point of view to find out why they sometimes ignore us.

Why we don't get more press coverage

Journalists are generally suspicious of evangelism: they tend to be dubious about anybody who feels they've got to 'convert' someone else to their own views or beliefs. The fact that the national papers try to do the same with their daily editorials is neither here nor there!

We also need to understand what constitutes news—from a journalist's point of view. News should be *immediate, unusual* and should *provoke a response* from the reader. If Princess Diana is recorded chatting to a male friend on her car phone, that's news. It's unusual, and provokes a reaction from the reader. However, if she does the same every day, week in, week out, it won't be news any more.

So we need to ask ourselves: are our evangelistic activities current? Are they unusual? Do they provoke a response? If we want press coverage for our evangelism, we need to give the press what they want. And if that doesn't fit in with our evangelism strategy, then we shouldn't expect the coverage in the first place!

But assuming we *do* want publicity for evangelism, how do we go about getting it?

Publicising a mission

Imagine you are holding an evangelistic mission. Your church is going to erect a tent in the park and run activities for teenagers. A band is coming to play, you're going to do some knocking on doors and a well-known evangelist is coming to speak. Now, these ideas will probably be quite effective in getting people saved, but they have little press value!

So what kind of events *would* get publicity? A church leader recently rang me asking me for advice for his church's children's mission. They were basing it on the Thunderbirds theme of International Rescue, which in itself was highly inventive. However, I suggested some ideas which would be positive from the media's point of view, as well as being good evangelistically. These were:

- A Scott Tracey lookalike fancy dress competition, with the Mayor and the editor of the local paper asked to judge the entries. This would create the following news story for the local paper: 'A hundred Scott Traceys descended on a church hall this week—for an International Rescue date with the Mayor.'
- A special party for all boys called Scott. Possible news story: 'Great Scott! Thirty boys called Scott went to a special party this week, to honour their Thunderbirds hero Scott Tracey.'
- A project to build a Thunderbirds rocket in a local park. News story: 'Thunderbirds were the theme in King George's Park on Wednesday when 45

International Rescue fans built a real-life rocket.'
- A parents' and children's party, with the showing of a Thunderbirds video, for children who like Thunderbirds now, and their parents who liked it when *they* were kids. News story: 'Thunderbirds fans both young and old got together for special party this week—and it went like a rocket!'

You get the idea? These events would provide easy evangelistic openings, and would also give the press some good story/photo opportunities.

So next time your church holds a mission, a project or a crusade, think of a catchy theme to it, and then start programming some events that will grab the media's attention. We're obviously not running our missions for the media's benefit—but they can clearly help us to get our message across to a wider audience. And equally importantly, publicity can help to create a climate of favourable public opinion which will ensure that our message is well received when it is delivered.

One-off events

The press are very keen these days to run items related to seasonal events. Christmas is an obvious one, but there are others, too, like Easter, Hallowe'en, Valentine's Day, Mother's Day, Father's Day and Guy Fawkes Day.

All of these occasions provide good opportunities for evangelism—and for the press.

One church I attended used a really innovative idea on Valentine's Day. We had several hundred Valentine's Day cards printed, in the form of a pink heart, with 'I Love You' written on the front. Inside was a love message—from God. The cards were delivered throughout the community on Valentine's Day, and someone called a week later to follow them up. The feedback was very positive—but equally importantly, the initiative provided an excellent story for the local paper.

When we plan our church calendars and evangelism programmes, we need to remember these special days—and remember, too, that the press are often looking for unusual items relating to them.

Healing meetings

Jesus found that there was nothing like a good miracle to gather a crowd, and I don't think many people these days would dispute the fact that healings and miracles are an essential ingredient in our evangelism.

Nonetheless, we need to be *very careful indeed* in how we present the supernatural to the press. Yes, a testimony of a healing can have a lot of impact, but I would urge churches to be cautious before inviting the press to healing meetings.

Why? Simply because, from the media's point of view, most displays of the supernatural are a bit weird—and if a journalist thinks a healing meeting is weird, he'll say so in print. Put yourself in the journalist's position. He may be able to cope with some raucous praise and a challenging talk; but people falling, apparently unconscious, to the ground? People screaming or crying when they're being prayed for? People speaking in tongues? Most journalists would react negatively to incidents like these—as do some Christians!

A journalist colleague of mine once attended a healing meeting which was handled very sensitively. He later described it—in print—as 'most disturbing'. And he was a very open-minded, mild-mannered person! The best thing that he could find to say about it was that 'people possibly felt better after being swept along in a tide of carefully orchestrated emotion'.

Now I'm not suggesting that we become so cautious

that we forget that Jesus and the early church performed most of their healings and deliverances in public, and dealt with the backlash when it came. However, we need to be wise. We need Elijah's faith before we hold Elijah's Mount Carmel-style public meetings! Bad publicity can hurt us— and the people who have been healed.

The new church's credibility problem

Journalists don't generally understand newer churches, and therefore don't find them easy to write about. They feel comfortable writing about church buildings, vicars, congregations, denominations and the like, because these things are *familiar*—even if they are sometimes as dead as a dodo! Conversely, they find it hard to understand that a church is *people*, that it has a leadership *team*, that it's looked after by an *apostle*, that none of its leaders are Reverends and that it is part of a *'network'*.

It could well be true that Mugthorpe Christian Fellowship is moving on with God, doing good works, seeing miracles and has the biggest church membership in the town—and that St Pomegranate's has been dead since the Jurassic era. In most people's eyes, however, St Pomegranate's will appear to be more credible, because it's safe, familiar and presented through well-known concepts.

So what can we do to redress the situation? I'm not suggesting that we turn the clock back twenty-five years in order to gain a bit of press credibility! If we are pioneering a new work for God, then misunderstandings and rejections are inevitable. However, there are some steps churches can take to improve their credibility. Here are some of them:

1. Examine basics like *name, venue, structure* and *times of meetings* and ask: are they easy to understand?

Let's look at Mugthorpe Christian Fellowship again. They meet in Bumblebridge Infants School Hall on alternate mornings and evenings, three Sundays out of four, and in people's homes in the fourth Sunday evening of the month. They don't have a leader, but Mr Ian Bloggs is the 'first among equals'—because he usually gets his own way at leadership team meetings and therefore has a leadership 'anointing'!

Firstly, what does the word 'fellowship' mean to the press and the public?

Secondly, how would a member of the public find out when the meetings take place, even if they managed to discover the venue? And how could a newspaper be expected to carry a regular announcement of meeting times in its diary column if they are different every week?

Thirdly, who is in charge? If a journalist wanted a quick quote from the leader for a story on Sunday trading, who would they turn to?

Journalists will feel more comfortable writing about a new church if it's in the same place at the same time, week in, week out. Repeated changes *can* give the impression that we're fly-by-nights with no real commitment to the community. Yes, we are committed to building dynamic, changing churches, but we must make sure we present ourselves as well as we can.

2. Make sure the church is *mentioned in the paper* every week—even if it's just a listing in the diary column, or a one-paragraph story about the appointment of a new treasurer. This all helps to breed a sense of familiarity.

3. Relate to *other churches* in the town. Many new churches have a reputation for being exclusive and people are suspicious—we appear like an isolated cult, especially to the press. So if there's a local Council of Churches or similar cross-church group, we should make sure we join, and that the press knows we've joined.

4. Work with credible *local organisations*. Our members should take up positions as school governors and councillors, or join the Neighbourhood Watch scheme or the residents' association. That way we achieve a genuine

respectability because of our wider community involvement.

5. Build credibility *in the community*. Social action programmes, play schemes, bonfire nights, carol services and the like help to achieve this and allay suspicion.

6. Build credibility with *people who matter*. Our leaders and key members need to get to know councillors, council officials, home beat police officers, social workers, teachers, school governors and others. Once we are trusted by the movers and shapers, the press will begin to trust us, too.

7. Affiliate to other credible *Christian groups*. Mugthorpe Christian Church (praise the Lord—it has changed its name now after reading point 1!) will do well to affiliate to the Evangelical Alliance[1] and any group, in fact, that is a credible force in its own right; and they should mention their affiliations on their headed notepaper, press releases and all their publications. This will help to avoid the appearance of a one-off local group with little or no significance.

8. *Avoid jargon* and in-words when dealing with the press. Biblical language is often out of date and difficult to understand; and some of the concepts are 2,000 years old, were written for a Jewish or Greek readership and were locked into a completely different culture. Why should someone in twentieth-century Britain grasp them? Most journalists won't know an apostle from an epistle—so we must avoid such words in our press releases.

9. *Be patient!* The Church of England still has a certain amount of credibility, both locally and nationally—but it's taken several hundred years to achieve it! We must have the mentality of running a marathon, rather than taking part in a sprint.

Jesus gave the Great Commission *to the church*, for the benefit of the *world*, not the press! However, the press can be a strategic means to getting that commission fulfilled.

---

1. The Evangelical Alliance is an umbrella organisation representing more than one million British Christians, churches and Christian organisations. The purpose of the Evangelical Alliance is to promote evangelical unity and truths, and to represent evangelical concerns to the wider world of church, state and society.

CHAPTER 6

PROPHET ... OR LOSS?

The Church's Prophetic Role in Society

Jonah the prophet could have saved himself a rebellion against God, a row with the crew of a ship, a ducking and three days in Whales if he'd issued a press release to the *Nineveh Weekly Echo!* A nice bit of hell and judgement and the threat of doom in forty days would certainly have caught the editor's eye!

And although God clearly felt that a personal visit from the reluctant Jonah would do both him and the Ninevites more good in this situation, the church of today would do well to recognise that the press gives us a first-class opportunity to express God's prophetic voice to our community and to the nation.

Now I'm not suggesting that we join the cult-like 'End Is Nigh' weirdoes who get on TV by predicting that the Second Coming will be next Tuesday—thankfully *after* EastEnders—and that the town of Much-Binding-on-the-Marsh is about to receive God's judgement and fulfil its prophetic name by sinking *into* the marsh! There are occasions, however, when the press can help us communicate the Day of the Lord's favour, or a prophetic call to repentance.

I'd certainly never suggest that we use the press instead of personal proclamation; but I do see tremendous scope for it to be used *with* it. Remember, our inspired 'prophetic preaches' on key issues may only be heard by the three ladies and a dog in our congregation, but our 'prophetic press releases' may be read by councillors, MPs, and perhaps even Government ministers and Royalty!

What sort of issues?

Let us suppose that gypsies have just moved onto some empty land in Mugthorpe. Their camp is only sixty yards away from some expensive residential homes, and local residents are in uproar about it. They are angry about the noise, about hygiene, about reported theft—and it doesn't take long before the issue gets into print.

Mugthorpe Christian Church, perhaps in conjunction with Mugthorpe Churches Together, may feel they have a clear duty to respond—both in private and in public.

The private response would be conducted with prayer and perhaps letters to local councillors and other relevant people, but the public response would best be achieved through the local press, radio and television. So the Mugthorpe leaders should issue a press release, setting out their position—and God's heart, as they see it. You'll find a suggested specimen in the Appendix on page 95, and such a statement would be guaranteed to get prominent coverage.

There are clearly many other situations where similar statements would be appropriate: homelessness, drugs, unemployment, abortion, family life, Sunday trading, embryology, pornography, homosexuality, the disabled, the environment, racism, nationalism—these are all issues on God's heart and I'm sure you can think of plenty of others.

Choosing our battles

Jesus warned us to count the cost before going into battle—and to sign a peace deal if we think we are likely to lose!

He said in Luke 14:31–32:

> Suppose a king is about to go to war against another king. Will he not first sit down and consider whether he is able with ten thousand

men to oppose the one coming against him with twenty thousand? If he is not able, he will send a delegation while the other is still a long way off and will ask for terms of peace.

We need to be aware that making controversial statements to the press *will* be costly. We need to pray and discuss the implications before we rush to the press.

First of all, we need to choose our issues wisely. Our forays into the press must be strategic and economical.

We must also make sure that our churches are genuinely qualified to speak with authority on the issue. Just quoting scripture and saying 'God thinks this is wrong' will not be enough these days.

We also need to check our church's credibility rating in the town. If Mugthorpe Christian Church are respected and well established, then people will listen when they speak—even if those people disagree; but if they have only been going a year, have six members and have had their applications to the Evangelical Alliance rejected seventeen times, their pronouncements on social and moral evils will be laughed at.

I mentioned in Chapter 3 about a letter which a friend wrote to a local paper in London. The letter prompted a mass demonstration outside the school where he taught, several public meetings, questions in the council chamber, a threatened picket outside our church, a malicious leafletting campaign and the risk of legal action against him—and he came close to losing his job.

Although God eventually brought a glorious victory for his church, the cost to my friend, his wife and children and the church was enormous. We were under siege for several weeks—from the press, from community activists, from the council, from the enemy. Some of our members found it hard to cope with and division crept in. It was a stressful time for the church, and it took almost a year to recover from it.

In retrospect, maybe that was a battle we shouldn't have fought—even though we won it! The price of victory can sometimes be just as heavy was the price of defeat, as many D-Day veterans will tell you. While I believe that Jesus is the all-conquering Victor and that we as His church have all power and all authority, we must remember we're still in a battle, and we are sure to pick up some casualties.

So we need to make sure that our membership is ready for a battle. And we must be very clear about which issues are *church* issues, and which ones are personal ones. While individual church members have the right to go into personal battle on moral and social issues, they should not expect the rest of the church to agree with them—or mobilise in support of them if the going gets rough!

Leaders should define church issues carefully, and should ask members in advance if they're happy to go public on an issue, and if they agree with the stance the church is taking. They should also spell out the possible consequences, loud and clear, and make sure that all the church's weak points—and vulnerable people—are covered. Prayer, fasting and spiritual warfare may be necessary—before, during and after the battle!

Coping with backlash

A journalist has the duty to get both sides of any story. The initial story about the gypsies may generate follow-up stories and letters the following week. The national papers, radio and television may pick up the story—they often do. The issue might develop into a long-running press issue in which the church and its leaders are called on to make several more statements, appear on television, or defend their position in a public, face-to-face debate with the local residents' leader! Backlash can come in a variety of forms. We must develop our arguments in advance and line up experts to back us up; and we must be willing to see the issue through. It's no good making the initial statement—and then running for cover with 'No comment' when the balloon goes up.

Reading all this might make you decide you never want to make a statement on anything more controversial than jam-making! Perhaps having a controversial, high profile will not be on every church's agenda, but we need to be aware that the godless issues are out there in society, waiting to be confronted; and maybe if we don't confront them, they might confront us and put us on the defensive. I'm a great believer in counting the cost—and then taking the offensive, on our terms.

Back to the future

At the moment, the church tends to follow the world's agenda—about five years later! We're currently hot on women's rights and the green issue—but we followed the world in tackling these subjects. We need to be setting the agendas, not just copying them. I believe God wants us to have that forward-looking role in society. He never does anything without informing His prophets—and sometimes we may need to go public with what He tells us.

John the Baptist is a classic example of this. He didn't have any hesitation in publicly rebuking King Herod for having an affair with his brother's wife—and I'm sure would have given a quote to the press, had they been around in those days!

Wouldn't it have been great if the church had warned society about AIDS—and launched ACET[1] five years before the disease struck! Imagine the lives that might have been saved if we'd gone public with the message: 'Stop loose sex now—there's a killer disease on its way.'

---

1. ACET (Aids Care Education and Training) is a charity which is now the largest independent provider in Britain of practical home care for people with AIDS and of school classes on AIDS, through their education programme.

I believe, and pray, that the church will begin to move in real prophetic power—not just by what we say, but in the way we live. We're people living under another spirit, and our lifestyles and attitudes should speak louder than words.

Our words count, too, however. We should be seeking to hear God, clearly and reliably, on contemporary issues—and speaking out on them. When we do, the press will be there to report what we say. I'm sure we'll be mocked, ridiculed and misunderstood; but imagine the impact and glory that will go to God when His word comes to pass!

CHAPTER 7

ORGANISING OR AGONISING

Setting Up a Publicity Structure

The leaders of Mugthorpe Christian Church read this book a year ago, took its ideas on board, and now have a high public profile. Their members have letters in the local paper most weeks, their events are listed in the information columns, they've run two campaigns with the local free paper and have had some of their people and projects featured on radio, television and in the press.

However, they've now got a problem. Their publicity-conscious attitude has backfired. Last week one of their leaders appeared on local radio warning of the dangers of having a Green agenda, while another was quoted in the local paper proclaiming the benefits.

And the press release about the gypsies went badly wrong—it criticised the council for not providing a site, when in fact Mugthorpe has *three* sites already. So now the council are upset.

In short, Mugthorpe need a proper publicity structure. They also need a press officer. Without it, their well-intended press invasion will end up in chaos.

The characteristics of a press officer

Any church planning a significant level of press contact should carefully select a press officer *first*. He or she will be the person in day-to-day contact with the press, radio and television. They will, in fact, represent the church to the press. So Mr Grumpworthy, who has a quick temper and only smiles at Christmas, is unlikely to be a good candidate.

Here are some of the qualities of a good press officer:

- They should be *chosen by leaders and by God*.
- They should have a *keen interest in the press* and a real burden to get their church into the media.
- They should have *writing ability*—a basic, natural grasp of English is essential.
- They should have a *friendly disposition*—to develop close relationships with journalists, editors, producers, etc.
- They should have *quick and easy access to the vicar*, pastor, leader or key members of the leadership team. Ideally, press officers should be leaders themselves; but certainly they would need to be able to represent their leader's *ethos and thinking* to the press, so that if a journalist wanted a quick comment on a given issue, the press officer could actually give one, safely, on the leader's behalf. They would need to know where the leader was most of the time, so that if a serious press issue arose, they could get a direct comment or word of advice quickly. They would also need an up-to-date knowledge of everything the church was doing.
- They should have *integrity*, so that the press trust them to represent their church honestly.
- They should be able to *keep calm* and think on their feet. A journalist might phone the press officer and claim: 'We've had a lady in the office this morning who claims to have slept with a member of your oversight team.' The press officer's *instant response* may end up in print. Someone who speaks before they engage their brain, or who gets defensive when put under pressure, is *not* to be recommended!

Now you may read this list of qualities and decide that only Jesus Himself would qualify! At the end of the day, we have to use whoever is available, but I would emphasise that it is safer to appoint a press officer on the basis of their character rather than their ability. Ability can be taught. Character can take years to sort out—and can land you in serious trouble with the press while you're waiting!

The work of a press officer

So you've found Mr or Ms Perfect and have appointed them as church press officer. What does their job consist of? Here are some guidelines:

- Organise regular prayer for the press in their area and for the ongoing publicity work of the church.
- Meet leaders of all church projects and activities and arrange for them to provide a regular supply of news and information, within a suitable structure.
- Write press releases about all church news and information, making sure it reaches the right person, in the right format, at the right time.
- Trawl the congregation for features/human interest stories and write press releases accordingly.
- Encourage and train church members to write letters to their local papers.
- Work with leadership to identify and organise specific press campaigns.
- Develop ongoing relationships with journalists.
- Organise training for church leaders who are starting to have regular contact with the press.
- Advise leadership on all issues concerning the press. This should also involve thorough *briefings* for leaders who are to be interviewed on a given issue.

Setting up a press and publicity structure

Here are some simple checks and balances in structuring our churches with publicity in mind:

1. Every leader and church member should be asked not to approach or respond to the press on *church* issues without speaking to the press officer first. I've known newspapers telephone five different members of a church asking their opinion on a subject, and then write a story beginning, 'Angry church members this week hit out . . . ' which implied they were speaking on behalf of their church. The press officer is likely to have an overview of all the church's dealings with the press.

2. The press officer should not issue any statements or press releases without consulting the leadership first.

3. The press officer should show press releases to the relevant people before issuing them, to make sure that facts are right and that they are happy with what's been written.

4. Anybody contributing to a story should be warned that the press officer's version of the story is likely to be changed by the press; and that a journalist may want to speak to them directly about it later on.

5. If a church has several congregations, it is best to have one press officer for each, with a press coordinator (likely to be a leader) overseeing all their activities.

6. A press and communications division should eventually be established, comprising leaders, press officer(s), people who design posters, write booklets and tracts and anyone who has similar skills, so that the church can devise a comprehensive communications programme.

Setting up a rapid response structure

There are occasions when the press want an instant comment or reaction. A journalist may ring the press officer or vicar and say: 'We're going to press in ten minutes. Can you give us a comment about Mugthorpe Christian Church's attitude to single parents who get pregnant deliberately just to fiddle more state benefit?'

Replying: 'Sorry, we can't help' might be represented as 'No comment'—and people will draw their own conclusions.

Nor will it be particularly helpful to say: 'I'll be seeing the rest of the leaders on Thursday. We'll discuss our response and let you have it next Tuesday after the church has debated the issue and had a vote.'

So how can we seize opportunities to get our views across quickly, and without shooting ourselves in the feet?

Here are some suggestions:

1. The press officer or principal leader should have power delegated to them to speak to the press in emergencies, *without reference to anybody else.*

2. The church should prepare, in advance, stock reactions to as many moral or social issues as possible. These should be thoroughly discussed by leaders and then condensed into statements of around 75 words maximum, with a longer version available if necessary.

Here's an example of a pre-prepared press statement on abortion:

> *The Bible—God's handbook for living—says that life begins at conception, and having counselled many people who have had an abortion, we know the distress the operation can cause. However, we would not condemn someone considering an abortion. Instead we would try to give them practical help so that the operation might not prove necessary.*

This quote represents God's word and God's heart—and you'll see that it's written so that *each individual sentence* could be used alone and still give a representative view.

We may need to update our file of stock reactions and add new ones as necessary; and we should always make sure the file is available.

3. The press officer and leaders need to learn to say 'No Comment' without saying 'No Comment'! They don't have to give a comment, just because the press ask for one, but there are different ways of expressing the fact. Certainly, saying 'No Comment' always sounds negative. It would be far better to say: 'Our church has views on this subject, but doesn't want to enter a public debate on it at the moment.'

I stress that these are the *basics* of how to structure your church publicity operation. Methods vary as much as churches, but some sort of structure and advance preparations *are* essential.

CHAPTER 8

NOW FOR THE BAD NEWS

Handling Adverse Publicity

Last year, a reporter from a local paper bumped into a member of a newer church which is part of the Pioneer network[1] and is based in Portsmouth. They knew one another already and had a chat.

The following day one of the church's leaders got a call from the reporter. The Waco siege had just ended in America and his paper was doing a story about new religious groups. Could he have some information about his church?

The implications were worrying. Was the reporter trying build a story that implied that this newer church was in fact a cult—just like the one in America? The consequences of such a story could have been difficult.

The leaders had a problem. If they declined to help with the story, the reporter might have concluded that they had things to hide, and said so in print, to lend weight to his 'cult' story; and if they answered the reporter's questions, they might have dug themselves an even deeper hole.

In the end they gave an interview, wisely stressing the church's links with the Evangelical Alliance and other respected groups, and its influence within the community.

1. The Pioneer network is a national network of churches in the historic, Christian and evangelical tradition, which seeks to represent the Christian faith in a non-religious and culturally relevant way.

Some damage was done, however. The quotes were used in an article headlined 'Seeing the Light' which referred to Waco and talked about newer churches in the area.

This was a classic example of how a church can be wrong-footed by a journalist. And it happens all the time.

In my days as a reporter, it was a standing joke in the office that the local vicar or pastor were the easiest people to 'set up'. They were so gullible! Jesus told us to be as wise as serpents and as innocent as doves—and we need to veer more towards doing snake impressions when we come to dealing with the press!

What to do when a journalist approaches you

Here are some guidelines on how to protect ourselves when journalists phone us or meet us on a formal or informal basis:

1. Journalists are *never off duty*. You may bump into them doing their shopping, or in the pub having a drink. *Keep your guard up.* It's easy to assume that you can talk without being quoted, just because the journalist hasn't got a notebook or a microphone in his hand; but journalists stumble on the best stories by keeping their eyes and ears open when they're out and about socially.

2. A journalist can quote you on *anything you say*—he does *not* need to ask your permission. You're on the record, at all times, unless you've built up a relationship with a journalist where you can speak 'off the record'—in other words, you are providing him with information, either on the basis that he doesn't use it, or that if he uses it, he doesn't attribute it to you.

Most journalists will keep their word and abide by any 'off the record' arrangement. But trust must be established, not assumed.

3. A journalist will not always reveal exactly why he is

speaking to you at the beginning of the conversation. So again, keep your guard up. They may apparently want to speak to you about an innocuous subject—and then drop a bombshell into the conversation towards the end, when you're relaxed. We should treat any call—even a friendly one—with a degree of suspicion.

4. We don't have to respond to anything a journalist asks us—either at the time, or at all! It's quite acceptable to say: 'I would like time to check the facts and give a considered response. You shouldn't construe this as "No Comment".' This gives you some breathing space—but you then have a clear responsibility to phone back with your considered response at an agreed time, even if that response is, 'We don't feel we have anything to say on this issue at the moment.'

5. If a controversial issue arises, get someone to witness your conversation, or get the interview taped. The sight of another church member witnessing the interview and a tape recording spinning quietly in the background has a very sobering effect on most journalists!

Giving good quotes safely

A journalist is quite at liberty to quote you on anything you say, with or without your permission, and one of the most frequent complaints you hear about the press is: 'They quoted me out of context.'

I rarely have much sympathy with people who say this! What they usually mean is: 'You quoted me—and now it's in print, I wish I'd never said it!'

We need to see things from the journalist's point of view. He's probably got around 300 words available to tell the story—and he may have other people to include in the article as well as you.

He will therefore have to be highly selective in what information he uses, and his selection will be based on *how*

newsworthy things are—*not* on which bits *you'd* like to see
included! So we need to learn how to give *interesting* quotes
which can *stand alone*—like the ones I used in the last
chapter concerning abortion.

Let's look at another example. Let us suppose you tell a
journalist:

> *We as a church are against homosexuality. The Bible*
> *says it's wrong. However, we must also remember*
> *that God does not condemn the sinner—only the sin.*
> *He loves homosexuals and so do we. We will always*
> *do what we can to help anybody who is homosexual.*

We shouldn't be in the least bit surprised if the paper
came out quoting us as follows:

> *We as a church are against homosexuality. The Bible*
> *says it's wrong.*

We'd be the first to complain we were not quoted accurately, but in fact, this isn't true. We have been quoted *accu-*
rately, but we haven't been quoted *completely*—and it's the
journalist's right and responsibility to decide what is used
and what isn't. So rather than complain, we must adjust our
comments. Let's rewrite the example above, making each
sentence self-contained:

> *We as a church always do whatever we can to*
> *help homosexuals, although we are against homosexu-*
> *ality. The Bible says that God loves homosexuals,*
> *although He says that the practice is wrong.*

You can see from this rewrite that each sentence can be
used alone, and still represent God's heart on the matter
accurately. Each sentence is quite safe on its own! Learning
to talk this way takes practice, which is why it's good to
have standard responses worked out in advance—and why

it helps to have training sessions involving mock interviews.

Points to be aware of in an interview

Interviews with journalists can take many shapes and forms and it's impossible to predict how they might go. However, there are some points which are worth remembering:

1. A good journalist will do his homework in advance—he will have researched his subject thoroughly. We need to be equally well briefed.

The journalist may also have found out some background about you, in order to put you at your ease and take mastery of the interview. There's nothing to stop us doing the same! Baroness Thatcher often wrong-footed journalists by researching *their* backgrounds. It makes sure that we enter the interview on an equal basis with the journalist. Nothing will surprise them more than if we offer them a seat in our office and say: 'I understand your wife's just had an operation. How is she recovering?'

2. Journalists usually list their questions in advance. It's worth asking them to send you a copy of the list, so that you can prepare your answers.

3. Try to be as courteous as possible—even if you know you're in for a grilling! A defensive, tetchy stance will produce offensive, tetchy questions! Journalists tend to be like chameleons—they blend in with the existing atmosphere. So you need to take the initiative in generating a positive, friendly atmosphere.

4. If the journalist is using a notebook, try not to talk too fast! Give him time to note what you are saying, unless you *don't* want him to note a particular point! It's in your interests to help him record the interview accurately.

5. Maintain good eye contact and use economical body

language. Journalists are astute and will be watching you as well as listening to you.

6. Beware questions that produce a one-word answer. For instance, if the journalist asks you: 'Did you feel depressed and miserable when you saw the report?', and you say, 'Yes,' they may be getting ready to quote you as saying: 'I felt depressed and miserable when I saw the report'—which isn't accurate. If the journalist uses this technique, challenge him! Ask, jokingly, 'You're not putting words into my mouth, are you?'

7. Take control of the interview. You know what you want to tell the journalist, so don't be afraid to steer your answers accordingly.

8. The journalist may have a photographer with him, or may want to send one along later. You should decide in advance whether you're prepared to have your picture taken and communicate your decision accordingly. Don't be pressured into posing for the camera. One church leader I know happily agreed to being photographed holding a copy of the Bible. The picture which was published made him look like a right Bible basher!

9. Make sure the journalist has taken his facts down correctly, especially if it's a complicated issue.

10. Make sure you establish the journalist's name and telephone number before he leaves.

11. Be very wise indeed before attempting any blatant evangelism. Be sensitive to the Holy Spirit—but remember, an attempt to convert a journalist would normally be viewed with the greatest suspicion, and might end up in print!

12. If the interview has concluded and you haven't been given the chance to make an important point, then insist on making it before the journalist leaves.

13. Never threaten a journalist. In the heat of the moment, it's easy to say things like: 'If you print this, I'll sue you', or 'If you expose the vicar, we'll hold you responsible if he kills himself.' But remember—comments

like that could end up in print. If you feel the journalist has mistreated you, or if you wish to explain some circumstances which might make publication unwise, then take it up with his editor. He's only there to report the story—decisions on what should be printed are not down to him.

How to handle a scandal

The press love a good scandal, especially if it involves a church. The church is rightly seen as being a highly moral institution, and so its failings will be treated mercilessly! And I've a sneaking suspicion that it is, in fact, God Himself who is sometimes behind highly publicised scandals. After all, He promises us that the things that we do in secret will be shouted from the rooftops, doesn't He?

Moral issues will inevitably arise. How we handle them can determine how much damage is done, but we must do all we can to keep them within the church family.

Let's assume that the press have heard about a scandal. What do we do? Here are some tips:

1. If a scandal breaks, a wise leadership will discuss what they will do if it gets into the press—and actively pray that it won't! Forewarned is forearmed.

2. If leaders hear that the press *are* onto a story, it's best to *pray*—and do nothing. Wait for the journalist to make an approach. Going to them may play straight into their hands.

3. When the journalist approaches you about a scandal, try to establish what he knows. If he's got all the facts sewn up, then there's not much you can do; but he might be bluffing you. He might have heard a titbit of information and is confronting you in the hope that *you* will innocently tell him the rest of the story. So when the dreaded call comes, say: 'Our church policy is not to discuss personal issues on the phone. Come round to see me and tell us what

you've heard and we'll do our best to help you.'

This response admits nothing—but calls the journalist's bluff. You're basically saying to him: 'Put up or shut up.'

4. If it transpires that the journalist *has* got the issue sewn up, we need to respond wisely. *Never* threaten him or try to persuade him not to print the story. Such an attempt may end up in print and make your situation worse. Appeals to prevent publication should be made to the editor, and only on *personal* grounds—that the vicar's mother is dying and his children will be taken into care if the story is published. Threats like refusing future co-operation with the paper, or withdrawing advertising, will be treated with the contempt they deserve.

A church's leadership will have to decide how to handle the scandal quickly, and will judge each situation on its merits.

The *first* thing they must do is to alert every member of the congregation about the gathering storm, get them to *pray*—and tell them *not to speak to the press under any circumstances*. They should say 'No comment'—and nothing else. Public statements should come from the leadership, and no one else. Journalists will often trawl round a congregation looking for quotes or titbits of information during a scandal. They might even turn up to our meetings. Our members need to be warned in advance. A phone-round would be essential.

As far as the leaders are concerned, I've generally found that a 'No Comment' response makes us look worse. We need to think positively and work out how to make the best of the situation.

It's wise to communicate by means of a written statement and hand it to any press outlet that *asks* for it; and it should be issued on the understanding that you are *not* prepared to answer questions about it. Few church leaders will perform well under interrogation about a scandal.

It's best to be up front and honest in our statements, to admit wrong-doing, and to apologise. Don't try to defend the person or the situation, or excuse the wrong.

Imagine the vicar *has* run off with the choir mistress. This statement would be suitable for the press:

It is true that our vicar, the Rev Bill Spudgrove, has suddenly moved away and is believed to be living with our choir mistress, Miss Anthea Horsepractice. Both of them have resigned from their positions in St Pomegranate's Church.

We believe that both Rev Spudgrove and Miss Horsepractice have done wrong, and while we still love them, we do not condone their actions in any way. However, although Rev Spudgrove's actions are wrong, he has been our friend for many years—and still is. And his wrongdoing does not negate all the good he has done for the community during his fifteen years here. Our hope is that he will face up to his mistakes and return home where he can be restored in some way—although obviously, his future as vicar of St Pomegranate's is up to the Church of England to decide.

Our thoughts are obviously with Rev Spudgrove's wife and children at the moment. We are doing what we can to help and support them.

We as a church feel we have failed the community, and would like to apologise for that.

The press will obviously be selective in the way they use this statement, although you can see that it has been constructed so that each sentence can stand alone.

Clearly, a scandal is going to damage a church and the people in it badly, but our response can certainly help God to use all things together for good.

CHAPTER 9

READ ALL ABOUT IT!

Producing Our Own Literature

As a child, I had two main points of contact with the church.

The first was by means of the poster. I used to walk past a Methodist church on the way to school, and spent months trying to work out what the poster on their notice-board meant.

It posed the question: 'What's missing in the CH– –CH?' The answer, was, of course, 'UR' . . . or in other words, YOU ARE!

Get it? Well, I did—eventually; but maybe that's because I'm a bit slow!

And then, of course, there was the parish magazine, which regularly dropped through our door—even though its contents were a mystery to me, since I'd never set foot in the church and so hadn't got a clue who or what the articles referred to!

Sadly, most parish magazines do more for the recycling industry than they do for the gospel; and some posters are so pithy they make you cringe.

I'm convinced, however, that there is tremendous potential for *good* church publicity. Church magazines and newspapers have an important role to play. People are used to reading free publications dropping through their doors these days. Why shouldn't ours be among them?

The church newspaper/magazine

An attractive, well-written church magazine or newspaper can do an enormous amount to help to improve our public image. They are also an excellent evangelistic tool: people who chuck a tract in the dustbin may gladly read a newspaper.

Nowadays, it is possible to produce a high-quality publication quite cheaply. So what are the areas we need to look at when considering a church newspaper or magazine?

1. Who is it for?

Every publication needs a target readership. Churches will have to decide whether the publication is going to be for the church members, or for the community. If you aim for both, you'll perhaps attract neither.

a) In-house publications

If the publication is for church members only, then the content is obvious: activity reports, lists of dates, some teaching, a few in-jokes, announcements of future plans, some letters (although not to bellyache! Complaints should be handled through fellowship, not in print) and perhaps a few pictures. Some gentle evangelism might be helpful, in case a church member shows the magazine to a non-Christian friend, but this should be incidental.

Church magazines can be typed and photocopied, or produced on a desktop publishing computer and printed, depending on your budget.

We need to remember, though, that local newspapers often get hold of church magazines, and go through them with a fine-tooth comb for story ideas. So we should not publish anything that we wouldn't want used on a wider scale.

b) Evangelistic newspapers

If your publication is for evangelism, then the content will alter significantly. You can use some powerful testimonies and stories of people whose lives have been changed by God; stories about all your church activities, together with information on where and when they meet; details of the projects your church runs, like play schemes, green initiatives; a map directing people to your meeting hall; a tear-off slip which people can send you asking for a visit/more literature, etc.; the history of your church and its role in the community; and a 'how to become a Christian' item.

These stories, together with pictures, could be presented in either a magazine or a newspaper format, depending on the area where your church is based. A church in inner London might produce a brash tabloid, while another in the posh parts of Surrey might go for a high-quality colour magazine.

2. Distribution

There are different ways you can distribute a church publication.

You could:

- put it through doors as part of a general evangelistic thrust in a community. You could then back the initiative up with a personal visit, asking people if they had read the paper and what they thought of it. The publication could provide good conversation starters.
- get permission to distribute it in strategic places like pubs, clubs, libraries, colleges, universities, doctors' surgeries, schools—the list is endless.
- get members to take some, or buy some, to give to strong evangelistic contacts like friends, neighbours and work colleagues.
- give them out on the streets, as part of your general street evangelism activities.
- use them as 'welcome' literature for visitors to your

    church meetings (see below).
- go for a combination of all of the above!

3. Cost and financial aspects

Producing a newspaper or magazine may not cost as much as you think. Let's give a couple of examples.

Printing 7,000 copies of a four-page black and white A4 magazine, with a couple of pictures on each page, would cost around £340, not including VAT.

The same number of a four-page black and white A3 tabloid newspaper, with a couple of pictures on each page, would cost around £1000—including paying a journalist to write it and design it and a desktop publishing expert to produce it on computer.

There will be as many different prices as there are printers; and VAT is charged on some items and not others. So these prices are only intended to be a rough guide. Remember—the printing market these days is competitive, so it pays to shop around.

Now there are ways of *making* money from newspapers and magazines.

a) *Advertising* is the obvious method. There are probably people in your church, and others, who are self-employed and who would gladly pay for an advert. Then there are other churches, and church-related groups and charities. And why not approach non-Christian shops, pubs, schools, colleges, clubs and organisations as well? If your publication has a big circulation, they might find your advertising rates very attractive.

If your church is serious about a newspaper or a magazine, you should appoint an advertisement rep who can go round finding business. You may be surprised how many potential advertisers there are!

The number of adverts will dictate the number of pages you have. Obviously, the more ads you have per page, the more money you will make, but you clearly need to have a good balance between adverts and editorial items.

A good ratio is around 70 per cent editorial and 30 per cent advertising on every page.

It should be possible to cover the costs of a paper, or even make a profit, if you've got a good advertisement rep who has the time to round up as many adverts as possible—and makes sure the advertisers actually *pay*!

b) It is also possible to *charge* people for the publication—church members would normally be happy to pay between 20p and 50p per copy.

Your church will need to make its own decision as to whether it wants the publication to be self-financing, or whether it's prepared to run it at a loss as part of its evangelism budget.

In my church—Revelation, Chichester—we launched a paper last year and have so far produced two issues, one of four tabloid pages and one of eight. Neither have broken even. The first one made a small loss of around £80, and the second one did badly, losing a few hundred pounds.

The paper was targeted at both church members *and* non-Christians, and was perhaps a bit too wide in its focus. Because of the financial difficulties, we have decided that in future we will only produce it for specific events.

Arun Community Church in East Sussex produced a four-page tabloid last year as part of a policy of distributing literature to their neighbourhood. It came out in April 1993, to coincide with a change in the name of the church. It went though the doors of 7,000 homes, with the aim of building profile and reputation and stimulating people's thinking about spiritual things and the Christian faith.

The feedback was encouraging. Arun leader David Thatcher explained: 'A number of letters and favourable comments were received, including some from local head teachers and businessmen. They commented on the excellent presentation, interest and readability.

'It is very difficult to measure whether the paper was worthwhile or successful. More people were actually attracted to the church and eventually became Christians through a televised service in 1990, which cost us nothing financially, but a lot in terms of time and stress!'

Arun are planning a similar paper in the future, but plan to put special emphasis on explaining in simple terms how readers could become Christians.

David Thatcher added: 'I feel that a widespread distribution of a well-produced newspaper, say once a year, to keep the name of the church in the public eye, is very worthwhile.'

Other church literature

One point that Arun discovered was that they needed literature—whether it was leaflets or a newspaper—to give their church *visibility*, particularly because they did not have a recognised church building.

Many new churches meet in schools and other rented buildings, so they face a challenge to make the public aware of *who* they are and *where* they are. So a publicity-conscious church should be looking at producing other kinds of literature to distribute to the community.

Let's look at some examples:

1. Welcome packs
How many people visit your church—and are never seen again? Maybe some of them are just passing through; but perhaps there are others who would welcome becoming involved in church life. So a welcome pack is useful. It should contain a leaflet explaining *what* the church is (in terms of denomination, stream, belief), *where* its meetings are held (including a map), *when* they're held (essential if you vary your meeting times), *who* is in charge, and *details of all activities* (i.e. youth groups, Sunday school, etc.); a Freepost reply card (which people can return to request more information/a visit, etc.); and a phone number to ring if they wish to speak to someone (preferably one which

isn't normally manned by an answering machine!).

People in the congregation should be appointed as 'spotters': they should be on the look-out for visitors and should offer them a pack *sensitively*. I'm no believer in exposing visitors in any way. Inviting people to put up their hands publicly while somebody clambers over ten chairs to give them a welcome pack, to the accompaniment of a round of applause and a roll on the drums, is enough to put them off for life!

2. Introductory leaflets
These are general information leaflets (probably the one used in the welcome pack) which are distributed in the community to help raise the church's profile. They can be pushed through doors, but a wise church will also get permission for them to be placed in schools, libraries, the town hall, the Citizens Advice Bureau, hospitals, doctors' and dentists' waiting rooms, old people's homes, hospitals, college refectories, pubs—anywhere where the public congregate. And remember, free newspapers will distribute leaflets to specific geographical areas inside their newspapers quite cheaply.

3. Event leaflets
These relate to one-off events like healing meetings, play schemes, jumble sales—anything that you want the public to come to. Remember to include the basic information:

- *who* is organising it
- *when* it is—date (including day) and time
- *where* it is—the exact address, and a map
- *how* to get there: details of public transport services and other route information
- *who can* come
- *who should* come (i.e. 'of particular interest to parents with children under 10', 'pensioners', etc.)
- *how much* it costs to get in, with details of discount

rates for children/students/unemployed/disabled
- *special facilities*—crèche, refreshments, wheelchair facilities
- *how long* it lasts for
- *a phone number* for more information.

Event leaflets are best distributed on a wide scale, around seven days before the event.

4. Activity leaflets
These promote regular activities like children's clubs, women's groups, pensioners' meetings, keep fit sessions—again including the basic details listed above. They should be distributed in places where suitable attenders congregate—schools, Post Offices, sports centres, etc.

5. Specialist services
Many churches offer expert services to the community these days—debt counselling, bereavement counselling, unemployment clubs, support groups, etc. Again, such services should be promoted in the right places. A door-to-door leaflet drop is unlikely to produce a response, but arranging for debt counselling leaflets/posters to be displayed at the Citizens Advice Bureau and information on bereavement counselling to be placed with the undertakers or doctor's surgery will make sure our services are displayed to the people who are most likely to need them. Advertisements and listings in the Yellow Pages and Thomson directories should be considered, too.

Leaflets, and . . .
Leaflets are important but they are not the only type of publicity that can be expressed on a piece of paper! I've mentioned posters earlier on, and there are other ideas, too:

- Advertising on hoardings and on the sides of buses.

- High-quality glossy brochures, suitable for giving to the Mayor, councillors, VIPs, etc.
- Car stickers, giving the name of the church and the date, time and place of meetings.

Perhaps you can think of others!

The importance of quality
The public are very design-conscious these days, so it's important that posters, leaflets and other material are properly designed and professionally produced. If you haven't got a graphic artist in your church, try to find one.

Television and radio

This book is mainly to do with our role with newspapers, since this is the medium where local churches will get most of their publicity, but we shouldn't forget television and radio.

There is a growing trend towards community broadcasting these days, and churches should seize the opportunities this presents.

Local radio stations will publicise many of the events, activities and news that would interest a local paper. They are always keen to pursue human interest features of the kind mentioned in chapter 2. And of course, there are always the phone-ins!

Even television is becoming more accessible. Many local stations encourage groups and individuals to contribute opinion items and true-life stories, and are prepared to mention community activities. It is certainly worth analysing *your* local station and see what opportunities there are.

Communication . . . a way of life?

Communicating with the public, whether by publications, leaflets or broadcasting, really represents an *attitude of mind*—and one which many Christians have to learn. My experience is that if you go into most churches and ask people what the biggest problem is, they'll say : 'Bad communication.' We won't be able to communicate effectively with the world if we aren't able to communicate properly with each other!

Jesus stressed the importance of keeping the lines of communication clear between one another. God told Habbakuk to 'take the vision, write it down'. Moses passed *all* of God's commands and instructions to *all* the people. And Luke was so keen to keep Theophilus up to date about the activities of Jesus' disciples that he wrote an entire press release about it. We renamed it the Book of Acts!

Yes, communication *is* an important part of church life; and as our churches grow bigger, we must recognise that lack of adequate communication is a real danger.

I recently visited a church leader who sent his *wife* a memo about a church activity! An isolated case (maybe!), but we must try not to let the vastness of our mission make us remote from *people*. We should follow Jesus' example. The directors of a big company might communicate with their managers and staff through memos; we should beware of doing the same. A phone call might take longer—but keeps relationships and people at the heart of what we're doing. Too many important moves of God have ended up desk-bound and confined to the In-Tray of church history!

Written communication is essential. Notice sheets are vital! But I would never suggest we use them as a *substitute* for a good, old-fashioned one-to-one chat, whether it's with a Christian or a non-Christian.

Communication should be a way of life, as a result of our love for *people*.

CHAPTER 10

TIME FOR A MOAN

How to Complain About the Press

I used to dread Fridays. The rest of the population would be happy that the weekend was only a few hours away, but not me.

Why? Well, when I was an editor, my papers used to come out on Thursdays. And that meant Friday was the day when hordes of angry readers would phone, or call in, complaining about the way they'd been treated in the paper. So I'd spend all day listening to grumbles and threats ranging from being sued to being given a belting from the reader's big brother!

Most of the complaints were unjustified, either on legal or ethical grounds; but the fact remains that from the individual's point of view, they still felt they had been treated badly.

I can guarantee that sooner or later, any church that gets involved with the press will have reason to complain. So it's best that we know how to go about it.

When we complain, our attitude should be to express our point of view, rather than score points, and to *win over* the person we're complaining to, rather than bash them over the head because we're feeling cross! You may feel better after venting your spleen on the local paper's editor; but remember—you're going to have to live with him afterwards, and there might come a time later on when you need him.

The journalists' code of conduct

The Press Complaints Commission has a voluntary code of conduct which most journalists and their editors have agreed to adhere to.

The code is very detailed—you can get a copy of it from the Press Complaints Commission, 1 Salisbury Square, London, EC4Y 8AE (telephone 071 353 1248).

It lays down standards of behaviour in spheres like: accuracy, the right of reply, privacy, misrepresentation, harassment, intrusion into grief and shock, and approaches to children and victims of crime.

A publicity-conscious church should get a copy of the code and check that journalists whom they deal with abide by it.

What you can complain about

1. A journalist's behaviour
Many newspapers nowadays don't just abide by the code of conduct but have a customer care policy which states how readers should be treated.

So if you feel a journalist has mistreated you in any way, either in an area covered by the code, or in another sphere, you have a right and even a duty to complain. An editor will want to know if one of his staff is not doing his job properly.

2. Something that's been published
It's surprising how many people are happy to talk to a journalist—but are furious, or shocked, when they see the finished article in print! There can be any number of reasons for this—maybe an inaccuracy, the way an article or quote has been handled, or the fact that you have not been given the chance to put your side of a story. Complain by all means, but make sure your gripe has a genuine foundation.

3. Your general relationship with a particular publication
Maybe you've sent 100 press releases to your local paper and none of them have been used. Maybe the local Methodists are getting more publicity than you. Or maybe the local paper is downright hostile towards you! You have the right to complain to the editor and discuss the situation with him.

4. The general content or tone of the paper
The church has a responsibility to act as a moral watchdog over the press. Your local paper might print pin-up pictures or use sexually explicit terminology in its court cases. Or it might print chat-line phone numbers, horoscopes and other harmful material. We have a right and a duty to complain about this kind of content.

How to complain

How we complain is generally determined by *what* we are complaining about. Here are some guidelines:

1. A phone call to the editor
Normally, a phone call to the editor should do the trick. Make it clear that you're *not* about to rush off to the Press Complaints Commission, but tell him what has happened, and ask him what he plans to do about it. He will normally want to investigate the matter himself and speak to you about it later, but make sure he does.

2. A letter to the editor
This is the next rung up the complaints ladder. Maybe your telephoned complaint has been ignored. In a situation like this, you may wish to write a letter of complaint. I stress though: *this would not be for publication on the letters page—* and should have the fact clearly marked. It's a private letter between you and the editor.

You should certainly complain in writing if you feel that the journalists' code of conduct has been breached. The Press Complaints Commission will only intervene in cases where correspondence between a reader and the editor has failed to resolve a problem.

3. A request for a meeting
Meetings are sometimes helpful either to discuss a church's general relationship with a paper, or to deal with a specific complaint. You could ask for a meeting to discuss how you could tailor material for presentation, to make church life more interesting and suitable for the paper.

4. A letter of complaint to the managing director
If you feel that the editor is not taking you seriously or dealing with your representations properly, a letter to the MD explaining the situation will normally bring a swift response. Remember, though, that such an action may sour relations between you and the editor, and so should not be taken hastily.

5. A complaint to the Press Complaints Commission
Such a step should only be taken when the journalists' code of conduct has been breached. The Commission's primary aim is to resolve disputes quickly and amicably. If this approach fails, they are prepared to investigate further and adjudicate.

The Commission produces an excellent booklet called *How to Complain*. It is available, free, from the address printed earlier in this chapter, and contains a copy of the code of conduct at the back. I suggest every church has a copy in its office.

6. Legal action
In extreme circumstances, an individual can sue a newspaper or magazine for libel.

Libel cases are heard in the High Court and bringing

an action is incredibly expensive—legal aid is *not* available.

If you feel a libel has occurred, then you *must* take legal advice, bearing in mind the old saying: 'It's as hard for a newspaper to win a libel case as it is for a poor man to start one.'

7. A letter for publication
You can use the letters page to air a grievance about the paper, or the way it has handled a story. If you do so, however, it's wise to ask yourself whether a useful purpose will be served. I wouldn't generally recommend washing dirty linen in public.

Recompense

In some situations, you won't be just complaining. You will be asking for some *action* to be taken in response to your complaint. Here are the situations where this would be appropriate:

a) when a mistake has been made
b) when the report about you has been misleading or distorted in some way
c) when a one-sided report has been published
d) if you or a member of your church has been mistreated in some way.

The press are far more sensitive to public complaints now than they've ever been before. The majority go out of their way to keep good relations with their readers, since if they lose them, they might go out of business.

Problems do arise, however—and most of them are genuine mistakes. If you do hit trouble, at least you'll now know what to do!

CHAPTER 11

IT PAYS TO ADVERTISE

... Or Does It?

If you fancy a night out at the pictures, the chances are that you'll turn to your local paper to find out which film's on where, and what time the show starts.

If, however, you fancy a night out at church, would you find details of the services in the local paper? Probably not. Sadly, many churches don't bother to advertise.

Spiritualist churches and groups like the Mormons and Jehovah's Witnesses are normally a lot better at advertising themselves in the press than we are—and they reap the benefit. A woman I once met wanted some spiritual comfort after her mother died and went to her local spiritualist church simply because their details were printed in her local paper's 'What's On' column. How sad that she couldn't find a Christian church in the same column.

The problem is that adverts cost money, and since most church treasurers make Scrooge look generous, the idea of paying to get our message across never gets considered.

So is there potential for using paid advertisements? I would say: yes, in some circumstances. The number one rule, though, is never to pay for something that could be printed for nothing. Most local papers print information free these days, so why bother to pay for a small ad?

The main advantage of an advert is that we can use it to say exactly what *we* want, and we can *guarantee* that it will appear. Here are some areas where advertising can work:

1. For a specific public meeting or activity

If you're holding a healing meeting, a play scheme, a community event or a mission, or any event aimed at the general public, then an advert can be very useful, particularly as a backup to a story printed on a paper's news page. Having both in the same issue will make sure the reader receives the information in two different forms. They are therefore more likely to take notice of it.

Some advertisers like their advert to appear on the same page as a corresponding news story. I'm not in favour of this. If they're on separate pages, the second insertion will remind the reader of the first.

2. For an important church landmark

Perhaps your church has just celebrated its 50th anniversary, changed its name, or recently ordained a new minister. These are prime opportunities for an advertising feature.

An advertising feature comprises a number of advertisements from different people, all supporting the same theme. They appear on the same page, together with some backup editorial material and maybe a photograph. You sometimes see them in local papers, covering things like gardening, spring brides, DIY or shops in a particular street.

So if Mugthorpe Christian Church is celebrating its 25th birthday, it might get ten advertisers to take out 'Happy Birthday' adverts in its local paper. These adverts might be from church members with their own businesses, other churches, the local Christian bookshop, or maybe national Christian charities or groups which had a relationship with the church. The adverts would be grouped together on one page and a story and maybe a photograph would be used, free, to make a page feature. Normally the church would be able to write the story itself, or certainly dictate what went in it.

During the Gulf War, I was editor of the *Enfield Independent* and recruited several churches in the town to take out cut-price adverts in support of war-related activities like special services and counselling. The rest of the page carried support editorial and the initiative was well received by churches and public.

3. Regular announcements
It is certainly worthwhile advertising our regular meetings, and if we have to pay, then so be it. The adverts can be quite small and needn't cost much. The best approach is to put one in for, say, six months and see if the response from the public justifies the expense. Bear in mind that such adverts do help to build up credibility and profile even if they don't put 'bums on seats' straight away.

It's also worth being a bit creative about regular announcements! A friend of mine, who was a wild evangelist, used to advertise Jesus in his local paper's 'Bargains for Sale' column! He worded the advert on the basis that Jesus came free—and gave his phone number for more details. He led several interested callers to the Lord!

Practical points when taking out an advertisement

1. If you are planning to take out a series of fairly big advertisements, it's worth negotiating a cheap deal with the paper. Nowadays, advertising is so hard to get that papers are often open to offers. Shop around.

2. Work out in advance *where* you want your advert to go. On the paper's news pages? In the 'What's On' listings? The paper's staff may be able to advise you. Remember, a *right-hand* page is always more likely to be read than a left-hand page. That's why you don't find Page Three girls on page 2!

3. Work out what you want to say. The paper's staff will normally design the advert for you, but advice from a Christian graphic artist is always helpful. Make sure the basics are covered—time, place, date and, of course, the name of your church and a number to phone.

4. Ask to see a final proof of the advert. Remember, you're the paying customer, so make sure you're completely happy with your advert. Check details carefully.

5. Ask for free editorial backup. You may have sent in your own press release already, but even if not, many papers these days will consider mentioning your event in a news story on the basis that you have paid for an advert.

6. If you are considering an advertisement feature, it's best to ask for an appointment with an advertising rep. Then you can work out the details face to face.

7. Make sure you get what you've paid for. If you've paid for the advert to be in this week, then refuse payment if it's left out. And if it's got a mistake in it, ask for your money back or for a free insertion next week.

I'm convinced that advertising can be cost-effective as *part* of an overall publicity strategy. Ideally a church will be mentioned on news and letters pages, in an occasional campaign, in the information columns *and* among the adverts. The combined result will be a church that is both high in profile and strong in credibility.

CHAPTER 12

KNOWING YOUR WRITES

The Art of Writing for Print

If you fancied meeting a friend socially, you'd probably pick up the phone and say: 'D'you fancy a cup of coffee?' If you *wrote* to him, however, you'd probably say: 'Would you like to partake in a beverage?'

An exaggeration, I know, but you get the point? Ask most people to write something and they start waffling—which is why many press releases end up in the bin and not in the paper.

Writing for newspapers is a specialist business and the groups who send in the most readable material get the most published. This chapter is a simple, practical guide on how to write press releases and letters that are likely to be published.

Writing a press release

There are several stages involved:

1. Identify the topic
After reading this book, you shouldn't have any problem in doing this. If you're still not sure, then turn again to page 1 and start again!

2. Gathering the information

A press release stands most chance of being used if it contains all the necessary information. Reporters are sometimes too busy to ring up to find out a missing fact.

Each press release must contain:

- Christian names and surnames of all the people in the story, with their positions within the church;
- ages and addresses of people involved;
- full titles and addresses of organisations involved;
- full details of events, including time, day, date and location;
- brief statements from *key people involved;*
- other facts that may be necessary, depending on the story.

Make sure each story answers: WHO? WHAT? WHEN? WHERE? WHY? HOW? WHY?

3. Laying out the press release

Press releases must *look good* to stand a good chance of being used. First impressions count. So:

- Type or word-process the release, using *double spacing* and *wide margins. Never* send in handwritten releases.
- Put your organisation's name, address and a contact name and telephone number at the top, so that the reporter can instantly tell *who* the release is from, *where* they are based, and *who* to contact.
- Draw up a press release template which can be used for all your releases. This way, reporters will become familiar with your releases.
- Put a note about picture possibilities at the bottom. Explain *where* and *when* the picture should be taken.

4. Writing the press release

The purpose of a press release is to *make your point quickly*. So you need to write *simply, briefly* and *accurately*.

Use simple words. Stick to the point. In general: *write as you speak*. If you're stuck on how to write something, say it out loud and then write down what you say.

Here are some other points to remember:

- The first paragraph should *grab* the reader's attention—otherwise they might not bother to read the rest. Ask yourself: what's the single most important fact in this story? *That* should be in the first paragraph.
- After writing your first paragraph, you then build the story by *amplifying it*.
- Then continue to build the story, giving the facts in the *order of interest*. So put items which will grab the attention of the reader near the *top* of your story, and the rest, like background details, down the bottom.
- Use sentences of between 18 and 24 words.
- Use one-sentence paragraphs.
- Avoid long words and jargon.
- Make sure your story answers the WHO? WHAT? WHEN? WHERE? WHY? HOW? WHY? mentioned earlier.

5. Sending the release

- Find out your papers' deadlines and make sure you send in your release with plenty of time to spare— around a week in advance, to give the reporter in each case plenty of time to react to it and follow it up.
- List the newspapers in your town, with the name of the reporter, chief reporter or news editor responsible, the paper's address, telephone and fax number. Send your release to the appropriate

person by name, either by post or by fax.

- Two days later, ring up and ask if your release has been received, and if any more information is needed.
- If you've asked for a photographer to cover an event, ring to see if one is planning to come.
- Try to keep in touch with the news editor or a particular reporter and build a working relation ship. Invite the editor to come and speak to your members. Or ask if a group of your members could come and look round the newspaper's office.
- Keep a record of every release you send. This enables you to check the accuracy of items that are used, particularly if there is a dispute. Also take copies of cuttings that are used.
- Make sure you send copies of the release to all the people mentioned in it, and your church leader.
- Think of other publications to send the release to, as well as local papers. Community organisations, councils, schools and other groups often produce their own publications these days.
- You can also use press releases to communicate an idea for a story. It's quite acceptable to write:

Mugthorpe Christian Church have a member, Mrs Agnes Buttercup, who is 100 on Saturday. She is celebrating by hang-gliding off Beachy Head. She had been a churchgoer for 86 years. We wondered if you might like to do a feature on her. If so, please contact us and we'll make the necessary arrangements.

Releases like this should be followed up a few days later with a call to the news editor, asking him if he plans to develop the story.

You will find a specimen press release in the Appendix on page 95.

Writing a letter

Letter writing is a skill of its own and other techniques are involved. Here are the main points to bear in mind:

1. Presentation
- Type your letter if possible. Newspapers will use handwritten letters, but typed ones often stand a better chance of getting in.
- Use double spacing and wide margins.
- Only type on *one side* of the page, and number each page.
- Put your name, address and telephone number at the top. Your house number and phone number will rarely be published, but are important for the paper to check that the letter is genuine.
- Put the date that you wrote it.
- Make it clear that the letter is *for publication.* Say so, at the top.
- Sign it at the bottom.
- Don't use church-headed notepaper unless you are writing *on behalf of* the church.
- Don't mention your official capacity or title unless you are writing in that capacity.
- Don't ask for your name and address to be with held. Editors normally chuck out letters from people who aren't prepared to put their name to their view.

2. Content
- Keep the letter short and to the point. Long letters are unlikely to be used. Keep them to around 200 words maximum.
- Be prepared for your letter to be cut. It's up to the editor to decide how much of your letter he wants to use, and which bits to cut. The best way to avoid this is to keep the letter short in the first place.

- If you are responding to a letter that's already been published, say so in the first paragraph: give the name of the writer, the date of publication and the subject. For example, 'I am writing to express my outrage at the letter from Mr G. Atkinson encouraging under-16s to have abortions, published on 4 December.'
- Keep your argument to two or three main points. Deal with them one at a time. Write as you speak—crisply and fluently.
- Use facts and statistics to back up your case.
- Don't be outrageous or aggressive for the sake of it. Remember, you are writing your letter to influence people, not to polarise them.
- Avoid personal attacks on people.
- Finish your letter with a nice sting in the tail at the end.
- Show the letter to one or two friends for their honest reaction.
- Read the letters pages in as many newspapers and magazines as possible. Learn what you can about letter-writing skills.

3. Submitting your letter

- Address it to 'Letters to the Editor', or abide by the instructions that are always printed on the letters page itself.
- You may be able to fax the letter, or dictate it over the phone. Again, instructions will be printed on the letters page.
- Check deadlines and get your letter in early. Respond to events *quickly*.

4. Statements of thanks, pleas and announcements

The letters page can also be used to communicate things to the public which might not be suitable for a news story. For instance:

Mugthorpe Christian Church would like to thank everybody who supported their craft fair last week. £200 was raised for TEAR Fund. We run a coffee bar on a Saturday morning in Bumblebridge Infants School—do pop in and see us so we can thank you personally. Yours etc.

Church press officers should be aware that these short letters help to build goodwill, and write them whenever possible.

Making a Start Right Now

You've read the book! Now what?

I hope you are now convinced of the need, and the benefits, of getting the church into the media, but let's not leave it there. Let's not be people who, after all is said and done, have said more than they've done! The challenge, as ever, is to be doers of the word, not just hearers!

So how do we get started? I'm going to conclude with the Ten Commandments of getting your church into print and on the airwaves, and if you work through these I'm confident it won't be long before you'll have a nice fat cuttings file!

THE TEN COMMANDMENTS

1. Give this book to your church's leaders (or better still, get them to buy a copy) and pray they'll catch the vision of having a well-publicised church; and if *you* are one of the leaders, pray the same thing for *yourself*!

2. At a meeting of the whole church the leaders should share their vision of increased publicity, warn of potential dangers and generally get feedback.

3. Appoint a press officer (PO) and get them to start trawling the church for story ideas and information items as described in chapter 7, and report back to the leaders in a fortnight with ideas.

4. Get someone to design a press release letterhead (see sample in Appendix on page 95).

5. The PO and church leader should arrange to see the editors of all local papers, to discuss story opportunities and how and when they like material sent to them.

6. The PO should brief all activity leaders and key personnel within the church on spotting potential stories/news/information items, and how to use these.

7. The PO should start sending regular press releases to all relevant newspapers/magazines/radio and TV stations. It's best to start gradually and build up profile, rather than appearing in a blaze of publicity and then disappearing just as quickly. We're looking for long-term *and* short-term results.

8. The PO should organise workshops to train people who are keen to write letters, then get them writing letters to the editor in consultation with leadership (see chapter 3).

9. The leaders should identify a campaign idea and fix a date in the church calendar to present it to a local paper.

10. Pray like mad!

APPENDIX

SPECIMEN PRESS RELEASE

Mugthorpe Christian Church
17 Holly Rise, Mugthorpe, MG1 7BU
Tel: 0444 556677   Fax: 0444 556688
Affiliated to the Evangelical Alliance and Mugthorpe Council of Churches

PRESS RELEASE
For publication in the first available issue

Mugthorpe's largest Christian church has spoken out in favour of gypsies who have set up camp in the town.

Mugthorpe Christian Church's leader, Mr Ian Bloggs, said in a statement today: 'We have been saddened by the enormous amount of prejudice that has been shown to the gypsies since they moved in.

'Mugthorpe has always been a town which has shown tolerance and hospitality towards minority groups, but this has not been the case this time. Since the gypsies have moved in they have been abused, humiliated and ostracised—treatment which would be rightly condemned if meted out to any other racial group.

'The Bible is quite clear that we all have a duty to show hospitality to strangers and people of other races, backgrounds and cultures. Jesus went out of His way to befriend people who were rejected by the rest of society.

'Mugthorpe Council should remember that they have a clear legal duty to provide the gypsies with a properly equipped site.

'We as a church would like to suggest a meeting with Mugthorpe Council and the local residents' association to discuss ways of helping the gypsies rather than continue a campaign of harassment which only causes more bad feeling, tension and division.'

For further information contact:
Press Officer: Mr Len Fisher, 16 Gladswine Close, Mugthorpe, MG5 8AU (Tel: 0444 123456) or Church Leader: Mr Gavin Smithers, 41 Underhill Close, Mugthorpe, MG6 1AB (Tel: 0444 654321)

PICTURE OPPORTUNITY
Members of Mugthorpe Christian Church will be visiting the gypsy camp on Saturday 24th May, between 5 and 6 p.m. There will be jugglers and clowns who will provide some free entertainment for children. You are welcome to send a photographer.